AMERICAN COMMUNITIES

We Live on a FARM

Cody Keiser

PowerKiDS press
New York

Published in 2016 by The Rosen Publishing Group, Inc.
29 East 21st Street, New York, NY 10010

First Edition

Editor: Katie Kawa
Book Design: Reann Nye

Photo Credits: Cover, pp. 3–24 (background texture) Evgeny Karandaev/Shutterstock.com; cover, pp. 9, 24 (barn) MaxyM/Shutterstock.com; p. 5 Mint Images - Bill Miles/Mint Images RF/Getty Images; p. 6 Steven Van Verre/Shutterstock.com; p. 9 Casper Voogt/Shutterstock.com; pp. 10, 24 (crops) bjonesphotography/Shutterstock.com; pp. 13, 24 (tractor) B Brown/Shutterstock.com; p. 14 branislavpudar/Shutterstock.com; p. 17 (main) Christopher Elwell/Shutterstock.com; p. 17 (inset) Anastasiia Malinich/Shutterstock.com; p. 18 Dariusz Gora/Shutterstock.com; p. 21 Chris Howey/Shutterstock.com; p. 22 holbox/Shutterstock.com.

Cataloging-in-Publication Data

Keiser, Cody.
We live on a farm / by Cody Keiser.
p. cm. — (American communities)
Includes index.
ISBN 978-1-5081-4209-6 (pbk.)
ISBN 978-1-5081-4210-2 (6-pack)
ISBN 978-1-5081-4211-9 (library binding)
1. Farm life — Juvenile literature. I. Keiser, Cody. II. Title.
S519.K45 2016
630—d23

Manufactured in the United States of America

CPSIA Compliance Information: Batch #BW16PK: For Further Information contact Rosen Publishing, New York, New York at 1-800-237-9932

Contents

We live on a big farm.

A farm is a rural area. This means it's in the country instead of a city or town.

There is a lot of open land around our farm. The houses in our community are far apart.

We grow plants to eat and sell. These are called **crops**.

Farmers have many special tools. **Tractors** are used to pull these tools.

We also raise animals on our farm. Cows live in the **barn**.

We get milk from the cows that live on our farm.

The cows eat the grass around our farm. They eat a lot of grass!

People from the city sometimes visit our farm. We sell them fruits and vegetables.

Life on a farm is very busy!

Words to Know

barn

crops

tractor

Index

Websites

Due to the changing nature of Internet links, PowerKids Press has developed an online list of websites related to the subject of this book. This site is updated regularly. Please use this link to access the list: www.powerkidslinks.com/acom/farm